Sleep Well, My Child
Hillary Will Be in Prison Soon

By AJ Aaron

For Pepe.

Good night, Daddy.

Good night, puppy.

Good night, moon.

Good night, stars.

Good night, my love.

Sleep well, my child.

... Daddy, can I ask you a question?

Of course, dear child.

Daddy, what is the difference between "extreme carelessness" and "gross negligence"?

Well, that's a complicated matter.

Really? They seem like the same thing to me.

You're right. They do seem very similar.

Didn't the FBI and the DOJ prosecute others who mishandled classified information?

Yes. I'm pretty sure they did. But they said Ms. Hillary didn't intend to break the law.

Didn't they prosecute and sentence a Navy guy when the "investigation did not reveal evidence that [he] intended to distribute classified information to unauthorized personnel"?

Whoah! Where are you getting all of this? I guess that's true and it does seem like a double-standard for wealthy, influential politicians.

But sleep well, my child.
Hillary will be in prison soon.

Daddy, what did Mr. Colin mean when he said Mr. Bill was busy "dicking bimbos"?

My goodness! Where did you hear that?

Did Mr. Bill really get a blowjob from a 19-year-old intern in the oval office?

Well. He admits the relationship was not appropriate.

Haven't a lot of women claimed Mr. Bill sexually harassed them? Did Ms. Hillary defend those women?

No, she didn't defend those women. She defended her husband.

Did Mr. Bill hurt Ms. Loretta when he visited her on that plane?

No. I don't think he was there to hurt her. He just wanted to talk about grandkids.

Will Mr. Bill hurt the girls in my class? Will Ms. Hillary defend him?

No, dear child. He won't hurt the girls in your class.

So sleep well, my child.
Hillary will be in prison soon.

Daddy, how much does it cost to play?

I'm not sure what you mean.

I was told I could have whatever I wanted from Ms. Hillary's foundation if I paid to play?

Well, there is still debate over whether those donations were illegal. And she can't give you whatever you want.

Can I be an ambassador? Can I chair the FCC?

Why would you want to do that?

I think they pay a lot. And I'd like to control the internet. If I controlled the internet, then I could make everyone love dogs and hate cats. That's better than owning the media companies.

I like dogs, too.

But sleep well, my child.
Hillary will be in prison soon.

Daddy, why did Ms. Hillary celebrate so many criminals at her convention?

I'm confused. What do you mean?

She had those criminal Mexicans speak at her convention and everyone clapped.

It's nicer to call them undocumented immigrants, and some of them were from countries other than Mexico.

So undocumented and criminal mean the same thing?

Pretty similar.

Daddy do you want other people to come here legally?

I do. I think immigrants that come legally to America are what made us great and can help make America great again.

Does that make you a racist?

No. Immigration isn't about race. It's about countries. You have to have permission to enter another country or you violate their laws.

So, a criminal, right?

Ok. Ok. I guess you're right. A criminal.

Does Ms. Hillary celebrate their crimes because she likes to break the law, too?

That's a bit strong. She sees it differently than you.

But sleep well, my child.
Hillary will be in prison soon.

Daddy, does Ms. Hillary want to bring terrorists to America?

Of course not. She despises terrorism just like us.

Then why is she inviting terrorists to live here?

She's not inviting terrorists to live here. She's welcoming migrants from war-torn countries.

Just like Europe?

Yeah. Kind of like Europe.

Do terrorists pretend to be migrants?

Yes. Sometimes.

How can we be sure we get the nice migrants? Do they have birth certificates, criminal databases, and records that we can check?

No. A lot of them don't have any documentation.

How many terrorists does it take to hurt me or you?

It only takes one.

Do you think Ms. Hillary will stop that one?

I don't think she will.

But sleep well, my child.
Hillary will be in prison soon.

Daddy, is it true that Ms. Hillary makes more for a 20-minute speech to a Wall Street company than my teacher, Ms. Green, makes in a year?

> Yes. Important, powerful people can make a lot of money giving speeches. A lot of Republicans also make a lot of money giving speeches.

Do you have public and private views?

> Well, I try to live consistently. So I try not to operate like a hypocrite.

Daddy, do you have one opinion when you are around rich people and another when you're around regular people?

> Well...

Does Ms. Hillary tell us the rich people lies or the poor people lies?

> I think she tells us the poor people lies.

But sleep well, my child.
Hillary will be in prison soon.

Daddy, will Ms. Hillary die if she becomes President?

I hope not. That would be terrible.

Isn't she really, really sick?

Her doctor said she just had pneumonia.

Do people with pneumonia collapse one minute and then greet little children the next?

I don't think that's normal. If it gets bad, someone would go to hospital to get checked.

You wouldn't go to a hospital if you were hiding something. Ms. Hillary is hiding something.

We have to take her word right now.

But sleep well, my child.
Hillary will be in prison soon.

Daddy, will you protect me from Ms. Hillary?